VERSE THINGS HAPPEN AT SEA

Dedicated to the men and women of the Royal Navy and Merchant Navy who know that half the sentiments expressed in this work are not true, but can't remember which half.

Verse Things Happen at Sea

An Anthology of Nautical Doggerel, Parodies and Other Previously Unpublished Poems

Collected and Annotated
by C. H. Milsom

A *Sea Breezes* Publication

ISBN 0 9513202 3 8

British Library Cataloguing-in-Publication Data.
A catalogue record for this book is available
from the British Library.

Published 1992 by Kinglish Ltd., 10/12 St George's Street, Douglas, Isle of Man.
Designed by Wirral Editorial Services, Upton, Merseyside.
Typeset and Printed by Comp Plus Ltd., Trafford House, Trafford Street, Chester.

INTRODUCTION

Sea Breezes was first published in December, 1919, as the house magazine of the Pacific Steam Navigation Company. In those days it contained a large number of poems, some which have been included in this anthology. On the death of the editor in March, 1937, the magazine was sold to Charles Birchall & Sons Ltd, proprietors of the now defunct *Journal of Commerce and Shipping Telegraph*, but had to cease publication after the October, 1939, edition due to wartime restrictions. The magazine was revived in January, 1946, and continued to publish the occasional poem but the practice has now ceased and poetry is no longer accepted. The magazine passed into private ownership in 1978.

These verses have been collected from many sources over many years, some from my own seafaring days of long ago, some from the pages of *Sea Breezes* and some from among those submitted to the magazine but never published. The best that can be said of their origin is that somebody, somewhere, at some time, sat down and wrote them. In many cases the names of those poets are not known and even where names are given the present whereabouts of most of the poets are not known, or whether they be living or dead. We hope that they will understand that we have published the fruits of their labour to ensure that their work lives on in a better and more permanent form than the tattered pieces of paper on which so many existed previously.

In such circumstances it would be invidious of us to claim copyright for this publication, although if any of the verses are copied elsewhere an acknowledgement to this anthology, its editor and publisher would be appreciated.

The line drawings are adapted from some of those which decorate *Sea Breezes* correspondence pages.

C. H. MILSOM

A Sailor's Life

Sailors are of the few remaining people who make their way in companies across the unsignposted face of the world with the help of the sun and stars, and spend most of their lives lying at the unhindered fancy of the weather. Their sense of values in human and elemental behaviour is therefore unblunted; they look on their existence as a long uproarious joke relieved by not unentertaining interludes of necessary tragedy.

Richard Gordon, *Doctor at Sea*

Rudyard Kipling started it with:

> Now this is the Law of the Jungle — as old and as true as the sky;
> And the Wolf that shall keep it may prosper, but the Wolf that shall break it must die.

Some time before the First World War Admiral Ronald Hopwood followed with:

> Now these are the Laws of the Navy, unwritten and varied they be,
> And he that is wise will obey them, going down to his ship in the sea.

The Merchant Navy's "Laws" were probably written in the 1930s although some of the statements made could have applied as late as 1950. This version was given by the master of the Thos & Jas Harrison heavy-lift ship "Adventurer" to his third mate, Mr C. E. E. Jones, in 1964. Mr Jones made a copy and gave it to Capt R. G. C. Riley who in turn passed a copy to "Sea Breezes".

The Laws of the Merchant Navy

The Laws of the Merchant Navy are intrinsic, pithy and plain,
Different ships may have different long splices, but the object in view is the same.

To the average dweller in cities they may seem insipid and drab,
But they're muttered by each hardy sailor, driving down to his ship in a cab.

When "Proceeding to join above steamer" and the journey takes most of the day,
Just pull out a pencil and paper and itemise all that you pay.

From the moment you step in the taxi, plus the beer of the evening before,
Put double the sum you've expended — you're sure to get half, if not more.

And when, to exact proper service, you lavish with money the guard,
Don't mention this on your expense sheet for the path of the truthful is hard.

Just lump it all under one item, "Transportation of person and gear",
And what the eye ain't aware of, the heart will have nothing to fear.

Now when you arrive at the vessel, and her marks of collapse show
    too plain,
If your father is worth a few thousands, put your gear in the
    taxi again.

But such is the stuff dreams are made of and you shoulder your
    bag with a sigh,
Her insurance is paid to the utmost; who'd worry if you were
    to die?

Though your room is no use to swing cats in, and the porthole
    is six inches wide,
"Accommodation for only one seaman" is a statement you may not
    deride.

'Tis stamped on the beam of your deckhead, with the crown of
    your King to concur;
If the Captain needs four rooms to live in, it is not for you to
    demur.

When the gang washes down in the morning and the water seeps
    gradually through,
Don't anathematize the shipowner, his ceiling may leak a bit, too!

At mealtimes when all are foregathered to dally awhile with a prune,
Don't force your point home on your seniors, by frantically
    waving a spoon.

'Twere better to sit with dumb wonder and slightly protuberant eye,
While the Master narrates his adventures (there are those who have
    risen thereby).

If the food falls far short of the standard, please remember
    before you complain,
That the steward will soon be retiring and must put something
    back for the rain.

Let no work be performed after luncheon, let no sound through
    the ship 'verberate,
For the executive taketh their slumber while their brains,
    undisturbed, hibernate.

But when this has all been accomplished and they waken with fur
    on their tongue,
Let your answers be carefully guarded, like a mine just about to
    be sprung.

When the vessel lies snug in the harbour and you stroll on the
    beach for a space,
Take heed of the nearest convenience, insobriety is not a disgrace.

Let no thought of the morrow disturb you for what, after all, can
    be said,
Provided you turn to next morning, though wheels spin around in
    your head?

As the end of the voyage cometh nearer and the world takes a
    rosier tinge,
Don't dwell too much on your pay-off, nor the subsequent glorious
    binge.

For it may obtrude at the moment when concentration is what is
    required.
It starts with a slight abberation, and ends up with you being
    fired!

These two versions of the chorus of a once popular song offer a good example of how words and lines can become transposed as memories fade over the years. The first is from "Sea Breezes", April, 1924; the second is of unknown origin. The "Ack" referred to is the Merchant Shipping Act, 1854, which introduced the compulsory provision of limejuice aboard British ships as a means of giving seamen Vitamin C to prevent scurvy.

O what's the use of grumbelling, you know ye get your whack,
    You sign it in the Articles and that's a _____ fack!
Then what's the use of grumbelling when you get your measly whack,
    Limejuice and vinegar, accordin' to the Ack.

You'll do no good by grumbling, you know how well you're whacked,
    With limejuice and vinegar, according to the Act;
You'll do no good by grumbling, I'll tell you for a fact,
    They can sew you up and dump you, according to the Act.

Poet Hugh J. O'Donnell was 92 years of age when he submitted these lines to "Sea Breezes" in March, 1988. The "Honorius" of R. P. Houston & Co was a vessel of 3,476 grt, built in 1899 and broken-up in 1925.

Voyage of the "Honorius", 1919-21

by Hugh J. O'Donnell

I'm on one of Hungry Houston's ships
    Loading cargo in BA,
She's homeward bound for Liverpool,
    We've been eighteen months away.

The cargo now is safe on board,
    We've battened down the hatches,
The tug herself is standing by,
    It's time to set the watches.

The pilot's ready on the bridge,
    No-one to see us leaving,
No-one to say just *"Adios"*
    Or a parting word of grieving.

He left us safely down the Plate,
    With a strong *pampero* blowing,
While on the dim horizon far
    The white-tailed waves were showing.

The wheel is manned, the seas run high,
    The old ship's hard a-steering,
The Captain eyes the wake astern,
    To see how much she's veering.

But when she starts to write her name,
    From the sea's resistless motion,
He hollers in sarcastic tone:
    "Don't use the whole damned ocean!"

There is no shelter at the wheel,
    No wheelhouse warm, or awning,
At night you see the stars above,
    Or a new day just a-borning.

It's four hours on and four hours off
    With wheel and lookout keeping,
So on your four-hour watch below
    There's not much time for sleeping.

The fo'c'sle is no home from home,
    Old two-tier bunks for sleeping
Where on a straw-filled bed you lie,
    With bedbugs company keeping.

She's just an old line cargo ship,
    And not a proud Cunarder,
We get no fancy food to eat,
    And we work a little harder.

The steward doles the rations out,
    He's the company's own jobber,
It's almost like your "pound and pint",
    He's a sailor's belly robber.

One day it's boiled salt horse we get,
    With a watery soup for dinner
And more pea soup and pork for tea,
    No wonder we get thinner.

There's always hash to fill the bill,
    Both wet and dry they're serving,
The memory of that tasteless dish
    Is not one worth preserving.

Of course there's other dish delights,
    To face a sailor's scorning,
Burgoo, potatoes and salt fish,
    The Friday's meal adorning.

Another loathsome dish we got,
　No simple words describe it,
No cook book holds the recipe,
　No doctor dare prescribe it.

We had it sometimes once a month,
　No menu had it on it,
The cook boiled all the galley scraps
　And served the crew Dog's Vomit.

We had dessert three times a week,
　The other four were none-days,
Rock Cakes and Apple Daddies first,
　The Plum Duff saved for Sundays.

We're nearly thirty days at sea,
　The weather starts to worsen,
As big seas wash the fo'c'sle head,
　The lookout man flees cursin'.

We have no fancy sounding gear,
　No aids to navigation,
A morning sight and one at noon,
　Give our precise location.

We're heading up for Land's End now,
　The weather's started clearing,
Some men have had the "Channels" long,
　They're cured with land appearing.

Now we're rolling up the coast
　With a friendly home wind blowing,
On shore a guiding lighthouse beams
　To warn us where we're going.

The Mersey pilot's now on board,
　There's a strong flood tide behind us,
The voyage done, we'll soon be free,
　No Articles to bind us.

We docked her in the Brunswick Dock,
　A fresh March wind was blowing,
There was no "Welcome home" for her,
　No hoist of flags was showing.

She now is safely in her berth,
　Her voyage long has ended,
The crew are glad to be back home,
　Not one of them pretended.

I sat a little while to think,
　What the future held, unknowing,
Then I packed my bag and made a vow:
　No more to sea I'm going.

Next day we gathered at the place
　Where the ship was paying-off in,
The nineteen months of wages due
　Would send a miser scoffing.

We stood around to say farewell,
　While some for home were starting,
A few went to the "Legs of Man"
　To share a drink ere parting.

I walked back lone to Galton Street,
　To the house where I was rooming,
It's just a sailors' boarding-house,
　On a side street, unassuming.

It's not a high-toned, fancy place,
　With a high-priced table setting,
I pay just twenty-bob a week,
　Three meals a day I'm getting.

There's nothing much for me to do,
　No job ashore I'm finding,
My pay-off money's almost gone,
　No ties I have to bind me.

In sixty lonesome days ashore,
　My vow begins to weaken,
I'm tired of a landsman's life,
　And down the docks I'm sneakin'.

I've roamed the busy docks for days,
　In Birkenhead I found her,
She's loaded, ready to sign-on,
　And I'll be an outward bounder.

13

"Sea Breezes", August, 1949.

A Sailor's Bill of Fare

Monday comes and while upon the seas,
All sailors true must have their pork and peas;
Tuesday next and with it this relief
To hunger pangs that solace of salt beef;
Wednesday in turn is but the repetition
Of Monday's fare without pronounced addition;
Again the steaming pea soup meets its fate,
Dipped with an iron spoon from an iron plate;
Jack pours it down and as he takes his fill
Grumbles and eats, eats and grumbles still.
Thursday and Friday are but still a repetition
Of previous days, without the least addition.
And as variety is always nice,
On Saturday he eats his beef with rice.
On Sunday, beef and pudding grace the board;
Pudding I say, but that is not the word —
No nice ingredients are required here,
Plums are too scarce and currants are too dear;
Mixed with salt water from the foaming crest,
To make it light and easy to digest.
Jack in a pleasant humour calls it duff,
And, forced to stay his hunger, eats the stuff;
But should he eat too much, I give you warning,
He'll want a dose of something ere the morning.
But if he's sick or with a colic blest,
There's salts and rhubarb in the medicine chest.
O happy sailor, how you should rejoice,
Though 'tis with you a kind of Hobson's choice;
No anxious thought of dinner on your mind,
The bell strikes eight and you your dinner find;
Again, at half-past five you get your tea,
And the next morning, as the case may be,
Should the remains your appetite provoke,
You get your breakfast or you have a smoke,
A sailor's breakfast gives not man the gout,
For, nothing left from supper, he goes without.
Perchance a slice of porpoise, flying fish,
Shark or sea bird makes an extra dish,
But dainties like these are rare and hard to find,
And so the sailor with an easy mind
Looks for the good time when he'll be at home,
And dreams of savoury dinners yet to come.

Origin unknown but the first of three parodies of "If—" for which apologies must be made to Rudyard Kipling.

The Company's "If—"

If you can keep your wines within the limit
   And never once exceed the twenty bob,
If you can work all hours uncomplaining
   And never, never moan about your job.
If you can answer silly questions smoothly,
   Politeness show to rich and poor alike,
Learn to flatter old and stupid women,
   And though you know they're wrong, agree they're right.

If you forget the things you see by moonlight
   In dark and shadowed corners out on deck,
Drink until the early hours of morning
   And don't become an alcoholic wreck.
If you resist the bold advance of maidens,
   Refuse to teach them what they'd like to know,
Guard them from your more immoral brethen
   Whose principles you rightly think are low.

If cargo slings go crashing all around you,
   When no-one does a single thing you say,
Yet cheerfully claim that you did all the damage
   When comes the end of each long, weary day.
If you can tally in a thousand mailbags
   And never once a single error make;
If all accounts will balance quite correctly
   And not one of the totals is a fake.

If your pay is cut for no apparent reason,
   But your feelings for the company stay the same.
If they cut your leave to two days in a twelve-month
   Yet you still revere the mention of their name.
If you laugh at food that goes from bad to awful,
   Smile on watch through snow, rain, sleet and hail,
Well, all I say is, "You're inhuman, brother,
   "It's men like you they want in Royal Mail."

First published in "Top Notch Magazine" in 1908, these lines were attributed to Rudyard Kipling but he denied all knowledge of them. They were reprinted in "Sea Breezes" in August, 1920, with a plea from the editor for identification of the poet. A reader then wrote in to say that he had seen the identical verses in "The Sydney Bulletin" in July, 1918, under the title "Seafarers" by Clan Fraser. The editor also received letters from different parts of the United States, each reader presuming the version he had seen to be original.

The Life of an AB

Shanghaied in San Francisco,
    We fetched up in Bombay,
They set us afloat in an old Leith boat
    That steered like a stack o' hay.

We've panted in the tropics,
    While the pitch boiled up on deck,
And saved our hides, but little besides,
    In an ice-cold North Sea wreck.

We've drunk our rum in Portland,
    We've thrashed up Behring Strait,
We've toed the mark in a Yankee barque,
    With a hard case, Down East mate.

We know the streets of Santos,
    And the loom of the lone Azores,
We've had our grub from a salt-horse tub
    Condemned from Navy stores.

We know the track to Auckland,
    And the light on Sydney Head,
And we've crept close hauled
      while the leadsman called
    The depths of the Channel's bed.

We know the quays of Glasgow,
    And the river at Saigon,
And drank our glass with a Chinese lass,
    In a houseboat, off Canton.

They pay us off in London,
    It's oh! for a spree ashore,
But again we ship for a southern trip
    In hardly a week or more.

Then goodbye Sally and goodbye Sue,
    For it's time to get afloat,
With an aching head, a straw-stuffed bed,
    A knife and an oilskin coat.

Sing "Time to leave her, Johnnie,"
    Sing "Bound to the Rio Grande,"
As the tug turns back we follow her track
    For a long, last look at land.

Then purple disappears and only blue is seen,
    That will take our bones down to Davy Jones,
And our souls to Fiddler's Green.

"Sea Breezes", September, 1922, attributed to "F.E.H.".

A Song of the Sea

Whether wine is in or wit be out,
    And the lazy old lugger is putting about,
For a cargo of cork or Dublin stout,
    The British sailor is never in doubt.

He can take you over the Spanish Main,
    Or nearer home, where the sailing's plain;
From the Firth of Solway to silent Seine.
    And round by the Orkneys to port again.

A rare old man is the deep-sea dog,
    He loves his ship and likes his grog,
And the only things he detests to log
    Is feeling his way through a filthy fog.

And when he seeks 'neath the Southern Cross
    The calmer seas where the waves don't toss,
His cool complacency suffers no loss;
    He believes that of Neptune he's easily boss.

So sing Hooray! for the sailorman,
    No matter his name, no matter his clan;
He sweeps the seas with a spacious span,
    And his work is fashioned on God's own plan.

"Sea Breezes", May, 1922.

The Old Whalerman's Song

'Tis well nigh sixty years ago,
On March the 20th day,
When we set sail from Yarmouth Roads,
And bore, due north, away.
A seaman brave our Skipper was,
And true as he was bold,
So off we went to the Greenland seas,
   To face the storm and cold, brave boys,
   To face the storm and cold.

The Mate who in the crow's nest high,
With a glass the sea to scan,
One day cried out, "There's a whale on our lee,
"A blowing at every span."
The Skipper he springs to the quarterdeck,
Says he, "Overhaul, let your main tack fall,
   "And launch your boats to sea, brave boys,
   "And launch your boats to sea."

The boats were lowered and the lines all stowed,
And the Captain cried with glee:
"Now bend to your oars with a will, my men,
"And bring yon whale to me."
We struck the whale and away she went,
With a harpoon in her tail,
But oh! and alas! we lost one boy,
   And we did not catch that whale, brave boys,
   And we did not catch that whale.

And when the Captain heard the news,
A sorrowful man he grew,
For the loss of his little apprentice boy,
And down his colours drew.
But soon a herd of whales we spied.
And took their precious lives,
And back we sailed to Yarmouth Town
   To our sweethearts and our wives, brave boys,
   To our sweethearts and our wives.

Singing "Aye lads, give way, lads",
We're bound to the north countree,
Where icebergs grow and whales do blow,
And sunsets you never see!

Submitted by Mr W. Jones who received his copy from a shipmate. "The writer is unknown," said Mr Jones, "but I feel he must have been a seaman."

> Have you ever been aboard a tramp
>   That's steaming down the bay,
> A'heading for some foreign port
>   Three thousand miles away?
>
> Have you seen the landmarks fading,
>   The coastline blur and pale,
> And sniffed the first tang of the sea
>   Against the fo'c'sle rail?
>
> Have you ever sat up for'ard
>   With your pipe stuck in your mouth
> And felt the air grow warmer
>   As your ship chugged slowly south?
>
> Have you seen a porpoise playing
>   As he cuts across your bow,
> The flying fish aspraying
>   Drops of silver on your prow?
>
> If you haven't sailed a freighter
>   Then sign on and go to sea,
> And before you've crossed t'equator
>   You'll have sensed its mystery.
>
> You'll understand why sailors
>   Find it hard to stay ashore,
> For though they're always grousing
>   They keep going back for more!

Submitted by Capt R. G. C. Riley who was serving as third mate in a P&O cargo ship on the Far East run in 1937 when he heard it recited by an elderly radio officer.

    A "Larri" boat from Barry Dock
       To Buenos Aires set sail,
    With tons of diamonds black on board;
       She did not carry mail.

    Young Billy was the Third Mate there,
       A farmer's lad was he,
    We often wondered why he left
       The plough to go to sea.

    The voyage took just thirty days
       To the Paris of the South,
    And Bill, his mind on pleasure bent,
       Soon for the shore set out.

    To the Balneiro beach he went
       One day to bathe and swim,
    No Sailor Town for Billy boy,
       The Arches weren't for him.

    The Mission girls adored him,
       He loved them all so well,
    For he knew they'd nurse him tenderly,
       Should he ever be unwell.

    The Flying Angel padre said:
       "Now look here Bill, my boy,
    "No Anchor Bar for you this time,
       "It's Bonzo's you'll enjoy."

    The local language puzzled him,
       He could not quite make out,
    When girlies said: "You likee me?"
       What it was all about.

    Now at last he's homeward bound
       With an amber tear, that's plain,
    To Hamburg and the Reeperbahn,
       To do it all again!

The Rev Thomas Hardy was appointed chaplain of the Missions to Seamen — The Flying Angel — at Valparaiso in 1907 and remained on the west coast of South America for 23 years, during which time his work on behalf of seamen became legendary. After further service at Sydney he was appointed chaplain at Sunderland and this tribute to him may have been first published in the "Sunderland Echo".

"Old Hardy" of the Seamen's Mission
by Sydney Brand

All up and down the oceans and by the cottage fires
They're thinking of "Old Hardy" as the missioner retires;
From Wear to Valparaiso two things were always sure,
A welcome from "Old Hardy" and the Mission's open door.

They brought their joy and trouble down the gangway, with an oath,
Unloading all on Hardy and he listened unto both;
Wise counsel for the erring who was heading for the sack,
He'd put him on his feet again and gently lead him back.

No bar to race or colour, no air of class or breed,
But everything obtainable to meet a seaman's need.
A sailing-night Communion or a parcel posted home,
The same kind hands arranged it for a man obliged to roam.

He bade "God speed" in wartime and calmed the youngster's fears,
"Reported lost or missing", he dried a widow's tears,
And he will be remembered unto all eternity
As "Old Hardy of the Mission" by the men who use the sea.

A "Sea Breezes" reader in December, 1954, said he had only just come across the song "Maggie May" and asked for the words. Capt A. Hodges, of Maryport, replied in February, 1955, with the chorus and said he first heard it while serving in the full-rigged ship "Aberfoyle" in 1890. Nothing more appeared until February, 1956, when Mr R. F. P. Halliday wrote from the Channel Islands with this version which he heard sung by an American sailor aboard the barque "Ville de Dieppe" a few years before the First World War. The reference to Van Diemen's Land places the origin of the song before 1853 when the land was renamed Tasmania and transportation ceased.

Maggie May

If you'll listen for a while I will tell you a tale
   Of what happened not very long ago to me;
How I was made a fool in the port of Liverpool
   The first time I arrived home here from sea.
I was paid off at the Home from a ship from Sierra Leone,
   Five pound ten a month that was my pay,
When I got my tin I grinned, but I very soon got skinned
   By a girl who lived in Peter Street called May.

   Chorus
      Oh my darling Maggie May, they have taken you away,
      To toil upon Van Diemen's cruel shore,
      For you robbed a lot of tailors and skinned so many sailors,
      That you'll never walk down Peter Street no more.

Oh I'll never forget that day when I first met Maggie May,
   She was standing at the corner at Canning Place,
In a full-sized crinoline, like a frigate of the line,
   And as she saw I was a sailor she gave chase;
So I hauled aboard my tacks when I saw her catch aback,
   Her signal hoisted up for me to stay.
Says she: "You're homeward bound so you'd better wear around",
   And together in Peter Street we'd rum and tea.

Next morn when I woke in bed with a sore and aching head,
   I looked around for my clothes but they were gone,
And with such a knowing stare, she said: "The Lord knows where,
   "You'd better ask old Uncle in the pawn."
When I heard this dreadful news I went raging in the blues,
   When two coppers came and took her right away;
And old Raffles guilty found her for she'd skinned a homeward bounder,
   And he sentenced her to Van Diemen's right away.

Oh the rain came down in torrents as in my pants and boots and socks,
    I made my way down to the Princes Docks,
But there I could not linger so I turned a comic singer
    And I made my first appearance at the Clock.
A crowd soon gathered round and to them my tale I told,
    Some of them seemed to think it served me right.
But when Liverpool more I go my pockets shall be low,
    And I won't care if they skin me every night!

Everyone who ever served in the Merchant Navy knows at least the opening lines of this one. Countless versions abound, all different and some with more verses than others.

The Lay of the Merchant Navy

You've seen him in the street, rolling round on groggy feet,
You've seen him clutch the pavement for support,
You've seen him arm-in-arm with a girl of doubtful charm
Who's leading Johnny safely into port.
It's filled you with disgust to see him grovel in the dust,
It revolts you when you see him on the spree,
But you've never seen the rip of his lonely merchant ship,
Ploughing fearless through a mine-infested sea.

You have cheered our Naval lads in their stately ironclads,
You've spared a cheer for Tommy Atkins, too,
But I've seen you in a funk when you've read of steamers sunk,
And you didn't give a damn about the crew.
You have mourned each ship that's lost and you've thought about the cost,
And it didn't leave you in a happy mood,
But though your heart was saddened and your mind was also maddened
You never thought of he who brings you food.

He brings the wounded back on a sub-infested track,
He carries troops and ammo over there,
He is owned by no brigade, he's neglected, underpaid,
But of his present danger he's aware.
He fights the lurking Hun with his little pip-squeak gun
And he'll ruin Adolf Hitler's little plan.
He's a corker, he's a nut, he's the bloody limit, but
He's just a Merchant Navy sailorman.

So when this war is over, don't forget the Strait of Dover
And all the other Seven Seas as well.
They'll be alive with men like these, bringing you your bread and cheese,
So you will remember, won't you? Will you Hell!

Origin unknown.

    Have you stood on a bridge at midnight,
      Not a bridge o'er a rippling stream
    But the bridge of an old tramp steamer,
      Deck laden and broad of beam?

    Have you peered ahead through the darkness,
      With rain-blind, salt-sprayed eyes,
    And cursed the Fate that brought you
      To a race with so poor a prize?

    Have you looked for a lonely lighthouse,
      For its welcoming, cheery rays,
    And known you've made a good landfall
      When you've not had a sight for days?

    Have you ever toiled in that turmoil,
      Deep down on the waterline
    Where the engines pound without ceasing,
      In weather foul or fine?

    Have you ever slaved in the stokehold
      In front of the furnace glow,
    Pestered for steam by the Deucer,
      You can drop but the ship, she must go?

    Have you stumbled about in the galley,
      Stove-top full of sliding pans,
    And wished the seven-bell dinner
      Would go 'mongst the also-rans?

    If you have you'll not doubt
      The story I tell,
    Of men who leave home
      To go live in Hell.

    Have you ever thought of the seaman's wife,
      An empty chair at her side,
    And the many times that she's longing
      For her man on the ocean wide?

    Have you ever thought of his children,
      Without a father's care?
    He's only a picture on the wall,
      A stranger whose visits are rare.

But maybe you think it's plain sailing
  Over beautiful sunlit seas,
And seamen do nothing but sunbathe,
  Fanned by a gentle breeze.

Well, they sweat to the bone in the tropics,
  They freeze to the core 'round the Poles,
And they're chased by mighty big combers
  That are hungry for human souls.

When a storm sets your windows to rattle
  And you growl that you can't get to sleep,
Do you ever think of the seamen,
  Out there on the rolling deep?

These are the men ordained by God
  To answer that prayer for you:
"Give us this day our daily bread" —
  Thank Him, but give seamen their due!

Origin unknown. Part of a much longer dirge usually sung in the "First and Last" to the tune "The Red Flag" in the small hours of the morning.

We live on scupper nails and bread,
  And oakum is our only bed,
When we sign off we still shall cry:
  "We'll keep the House Flag flying high!"

"Sea Breezes", April, 1922; said to have stemmed from "an ancient maritime leaflet" and attributed to "The Man on the Lookout".

An Old Shellback on His Life at Sea

In eighteen hundred and thirty-one, I first set out to sea,
A little Jammy cabin-boy no higher than your knee;
I had my little bag of clothes, and a proper sailor's knife—
Indeed, I held more property than I had done all my life.
Away I went on board a ship, she was lying at the quay,
The pilot came, unmoored her, and off we went to sea.

The wind blew hard, the sea ran high, the ship began to roll!
Water rushing fore and aft, the decks were full of coal.
Wet and cold I scrambled aft and made my way below,
And vowed if I got home again I never more would go.
Daylight came, night again, black as it was before,
There I lay, all wet and cold, upon the cabin floor.

The Captain often looked at me, and with a smile he said:
"Boy, you look as happy as though your passage had been paid."
The sea got smooth, and land in sight, I was told to go on deck,
Or by that name they use so much they would break my little neck.
I scrambled on the deck again, my little legs were weak,
My head runned round, I could not stand there, I lost my feet.

The Mate with a pair of big seaboots, he kicked me on the head,
"Get up, you little lazy whelp," this cruel monster said;
Three years I suffered much from Master, Mate, and men.
Thank God, the boys cannot be used so cruel now as then;
I have served my fifty years at sea and passed through every grade,
I've been master of steam and sailers in coast and foreign trade.

I never lost a vessel all these years at sea;
Nor did I ever down a man that sailed along with me.
I am now grown old, my sight is dim, I cannot go no more,
I find it hard for a sailor to live upon the shore;
Had I served my Queen for fifty years, so honest and so true,
In my old age I would not have been so poor as I am now.

Ships and Cargoes

Passengers and mail can go by Wells Fargo,
But it takes a ship to carry cargo.
                                Origin unknown

"Sea Breezes", February, 1923, but attributed to "A.W." in the Liverpool "Courier".

Ode to Tramp Steamers

Tramps, tramps, tramps — aye, by the thousand,
   Out from Mersey, Thames, and Tees,
Deep, green water at your bows, and
    Plod, plod, plodding at your ease
    At a paltry speed, in knots,
    To most God-forsaken spots
Up and down and round about the salty seas.

Black, grim'd, filthy black and gritty,
   (Just like vagrants of the road)
Children of the very city
    On whose river once you rode
    In a manner proud and quaint,
    With your gay and gaudy paint,
And the saucy independence that you show'd.

Guess you're rich — as rich as Crœsus,
   Now you've finished roving round;
Guess, too, somebody'll fleece us
    O'er what you have sought and found —
    All those odds and ends of stuff
    That you shipped from yonder lough,
Or some stinking foreign quay or tropic sound.

Off again! but first to Garston,
   Coals aboard e'er evening star,
And, by daybreak, you have pass'd on
    Far, far, far beyond the Bar;
    In a month or so, perhaps,
    You'll be trading with the Japs,
Or a-steaming through the mighty Panama!

Thanks, ye tramps, for your example!
   If Life's battle can be won,
I, and many a human tramp'll
    Strive to fight as you have done.
    Aye, we'll plod, and plod and plod
    'Long the stony ways of God,
And with courage go a-tramping, tramping on!

This poem exists on a properly printed sheet and is almost certainly American in origin although the sentiments expressed echo those of many who served in "Liberty" ships.

"Liberty" Ship

Laden deep from lands afar,
The "Liberty" stands at the pilot's bar,
A rusty tramp that has euchered fate,
Heaves in the swell off the Golden Gate.

Yes, she's "Liberty" built in twenty days,
One of the hundreds that slipped the ways.
A champagne bottle, an unknown name.
And no designs on future fame.

She was laden deep with goods of war.
Below her marks both aft and fore,
And as if to tempt the hand of fate,
Her decks were piled with 'plane and crate.

Each time she dives she shudders free
And pounds her way through the angry sea;
There are those who would sneer at these,
But they have never sailed the seas.

The "Liberty" tramp, the butt of jests,
Can-opener ship, and all the rest.
An ugly duckling, a rusty pot,
Waiting for the wrecker's lot.

So now, dear lass, don't mind the name,
Your endless miles have won you fame,
From tropic heat to Arctic flow,
There's not a sea lane you don't know.

The Murmansk run, and Attu's shore,
Salerno beach-head and many more,
After the Naval gunfire shook,
You were the first to drop the hook.

Why, there's not a cargo great or small
But a "Liberty" tramp has carried them all,
High test gas and TNT
From Guadalcanal to Tripoli.

You are the prey of the U-boat pack
That lurks on the ocean's merchant track,
Your hulls lay blasted on ocean's bed,
While your sister ships sail overhead.

We've trod your decks, we're proud to tell,
You've sailed us in and out of Hell,
We've cursed you, and we've praised you, too.
As sailormen so often do.

We'll drink a glass at the Mariner's Bar,
To you, good ship, so there you are,
A merchant ship, a "Liberty",
Another tramp upon the sea.

But hark, that is the stand-by bell.
The pilot's boarded, all is well,
Another trip comes to its end,
We say farewell to you, my friend.

A week ashore, we'll hear the call,
And then, the sailor's Shipping Hall,
A sailor's life is bold and free
"Oh Hell! Another 'Liberty' "

Based loosely on the hymn "Blessèd Assurance" by Frances Jane van Alstyne, considerably cleaned up from the original Royal Navy version.

Landing Craft, Infantry

She's a wonderful ship, through the sea she will flip,
   She's sailing by night and by day,
And when she's in motion she's the pride of the ocean,
   You can't see her bottom for spray.
Side, side, LCI side, the Skipper looks on her with pride,
   He'd fall in a faint if you dared scratch the paint
On the side of his LCI side.

   This is my story, this is my song,
     We've been in the Andrew too bloomin' long,
    So roll on the *Nelson*, the *Rodney*, *Renown*,
      These flat-bottomed blighters are getting me down.

The Blue Funnel cargo liner "Stentor" was torpedoed in the North Atlantic on October 27, 1942, and sank in eight minutes with the loss of 45 passengers and crew members. The corvette "Woodruff" picked up 202 survivors, including the author who was in command of the troops on board. Five days later, because the "Woodruff" was running short of food with so many extra mouths to feed, 100 survivors were transferred to the destroyer "Ramsey".

This further parody on Kipling's "If —" was submitted by Mr R. Borrer, senior radio officer of the "Stentor", and was published in "Sea Breezes" in June, 1990, together with Mr Borrer's account of the loss of the ship.

A Stentorian "If —"
by H. C. Wheatley

If you can earn your leave and start to take it
   In a cabin six-foot three by four-foot four,
Piled up with kit as full as you can make it
   With not a chance of getting out the door.
If you can steam along and keep in station
   With other ships, whose company seems bright,
And have your weekly bath with jubilation,
   Then get torpedoed, suddenly, at night.

If you "Abandon ship" — not getting frantic
   Because the ship's boats all have gone away,
And step into the stormy grey Atlantic
   Still waiting for tomorrow's break of day.
If you can swim in palm oil and not drink it
   And, waiting to be rescued, try to laugh,
Then see the *Woodruff* coming and not think it
   A U-boat coming up to straffe.

If you can be one of those wet survivors
   That's picked up in the dark, from out of the sea,
And given, without stint, such grand revivers,
   By everyone, from Captain to AB.
If you can stand the corvette's giddy motion
   And "Action Stations" seven times a night,
While charging at full speed straight through the ocean
   Though seasick, answering back "I'm quite all right".

If you can be transhipped in just a thimble
   From egg-shell craft to one of lighter trim,
By scrambling overside — Oh, how so nimble,

>   To board the *Ramsey* and not have to swim.
> If you can enter in that place marked "Captain",
>   And push that poor unfortunate on deck.
> And while sweet sleep you lay so soundly wrapt in,
>   You never hear him say he likes your neck.
>
> If you can eat the First Lieutenant's dinner
>   Then ask him if you're getting in the way,
> And get a beaming smile from that poor sinner,
>   And the hope that you have a pleasant day.
> If you can join the wardroom of the *Ramsey*
>   And, after all your trials, still show pluck.
> Then, Sir, your life has been extremely jammy,
>   In fact, Sir, you've had all the ruddy luck.

Based on the hymn "O God Our Help in Ages Past" by Isaac Watts.

> Esso our help in cargoes past,
>   Our hope for ports to come,
> Expedite our cargoes fast,
>   And keep us on the run.
>
> Despite the straining of our pumps,
>   Thy lines shall dwell secure,
> Sufficient fifty pounds alone
>   Our bonuses are sure.
>
> Stretch out thine arm from Dorland House
>   And make our strippers strong,
> Then help us when the pressure fails,
>   To pass the buck along.
>
> And those that sit aloft with thee,
>   Make wise in water-tubes,
> That we may strive unceasingly,
>   To carry Essolubes.
>
> Be with us when our breakers arc
>   And feed pumps go awry,
> Be with us in the Lago Club,
>   Be with us when we die.
>
> And if we serve thee well in life,
>   When Gabriel's trumpets sound,
> If we, in Heaven's harbour berth,
>   Forget to turn around.

The Pacific Steam Navigation Company's liner "Ortega", 7,920 grt, built 1906, embarked 300 French reservists and their families at Valparaiso, Chile, on September 12, 1914, coaled at Coronel and sailed for Liverpool by way of Cape Horn on September 16. Three days later she was intercepted by the German light cruiser "Dresden" and ordered to stop but Chief Engineer R. Alles worked the 14-knot ship up to 18 knots and her master, Capt D. R. Kinnier, turned her into the Nelson Strait, an uncharted and believedly unnavigable passage through the Queen Adelaide Archipelago for a vessel drawing 26ft.

With a ship's boat ahead of her taking soundings and relaying the depth by semaphore, the "Ortega" crept through the tortuous channels by daylight and anchored at night. She finally emerged into the familiar Strait of Magellan to find waiting for her, not the "Dresden" but the Chilean destroyer "Almirante Lynch" which had been despatched to search for survivors, the "Ortega" having been reported sunk. Capt Kinnier was awarded the DSC in recognition of his magnificent seamanship and his ship lasted until 1927 when she was broken-up. The "Dresden" was shelled into submission on March 14, 1915, by the British cruisers "Kent" and "Glasgow" and the AMC "Orama" and was scuttled to avoid capture.

These verses first appeared in the Christmas, 1914, number of the magazine "John Bull". When "Sea Breezes" was launched as the house magazine of the Pacific Steam Navigation Company in December, 1919, they were considered appropriate for inclusion in the first issue.

A Ballad of the "Ortega"

by "Ricardo"

The ship she was a British ship, the Union Jack she flew;
She sailed the broad Pacific main and danced it through the blue,
Until a German cruiser came, so big and full of brag,
Said Captain Sauerkraut, "Just heave to, haul down the British flag!"

The ship she was a steamer old, built for a peaceful trade;
The cruiser, mounting heavy guns, was armoured and new made.
The ship she wasn't very fast, 'bout 14 knots an hour,
The German, doing twenty-one, had got her in his power.

At least that's what the German thought, his smile was very broad.
He said: "Three hundred fighting men of France you have on board,
"That's why I bid you strike your flag, my pris'ners you must be
"And France and England, both at once, must bow to Germany."

That those three hundred Frenchmen were aboard the ship 'tis true,
But also, let it be explained, so was a British crew.
Another little item that the German quite forgot,
The ship she had a Britisher as captain of the lot.

The Captain, ordered to give in, he answered, "Bless your eyes!
"Before this ship surrenders I'll see you in Paradise!"
The German's dignity was hurt, he let some curses slip,
And then his guns they opened fire to sink that trading ship.

The Captain called for volunteers and said in happy tones:
"Out here those guns of his will send us all to Davy Jones,
"But if, my men, you'll stoke the ship I'll hug the rocky shore
"And take the old *Ortega* where no boat has been before."

They stripped and stoked, the ship's speed was whacked up to eighteen knots.
The German guns, so close behind, sent in a storm of shots.
And Sauerkraut cried, "That Englishman is crazy, I expect,
"For if he makes for Nelson's Straits, *mein Gott,* he will be wrecked!"

Slap in the straits the Captain steamed, shoals, reefs, rocks, snags were there;
No chart to guide him, yet he laughed: "Now follow if you dare!"
Cried Sauerkraut, "Yield, don't take the straits, it's death for all of you!"
The Captain said, "So long, old chap, this ship is going through!"

And through she went, where no ship sailed since first the world began,
With all her precious passengers, the boat to safety ran.
The German next time won't be half so cocksure of his plan,
Not when a vessel's skippered by a British sailorman.

A lady passenger aboard the Pacific Steam Navigation Company's "Iberia" in 1897 so impressed the master, Capt F. E. Kite, with her intelligent interest in nautical matters that he created her honorary fifth officer. The lady in turn was so impressed with the "Iberia" and her crew that she wrote the following poem and presented it to Capt Kite. When Capt Kite retired as commodore of the line he offered it to "Sea Breezes", where it was published in March, 1923.

Farewell to the "Iberia"

Wistfully silent I stand on the quay,
   And my heart it is aching so sadly;
For this is the hour which takes thee from me,
   And oh I shall miss thee right badly.

Iberia, words cannot possibly say
   One quarter of all that I feel,
I love thee, old ship, from thy bow to thy stern,
   From thy lofty truck to thy keel.

'Tis true thou art ancient, but still wondrous fair,
   In delicate grace of outline,
In absolute symmetry none can compare,
   Be the new steamers ever so fine.

The storms thou hast weathered, the seas thou hast crossed,
   The gales thou has had to endure,
Where other ships foundered, or lay tempest-tossed,
   Thou borest thy cargo secure.

Of Captain and Officers well may'st thou boast,
   One traces a masterly hand
In the way thou art steered round that treacherous coast,
   Through Magellan's swift straits, too, 'tis grand.

Such absolute vigilance, morning and night,
   Such discipline, steady and clear;
To watch how thy engines are worked is a sight,
   Right skilled is thy Chief Engineer.

For thirty-nine days since we left England's shore,
   Have I roamed o'er thy decks at my will,
Cruel thought that perhaps I shall tread them no more,
   Oh that on board I were still.

There is so much to learn in a nautical line,
    A life so entirely new,
The way that they worked thee, old ship, it was fine,
    The Captain, his staff and the crew.

Thy steering was really a wonderful sight,
    Thy watches so carefully kept;
All in such order, from morning 'till night,
    I wondered sometimes when they slept.

Of milit'ry discipline, much I have seen,
    And well know their words of command,
But the rigours of sea life (until one has been
    And proved them) one can't understand.

Such quickness of eye, such immediate resource,
    Decision so prompt and so sure;
All hardships are borne as a matter of course,
    It's wonderful what they endure.

This science 'gainst nature, perpetual war
    With the elements, time without end;
How little we know, we who live on the shore,
    The forces they have to contend.

Adverse winds, sunken reefs, cross tides, sudden squalls
    'Tis a battle wherever they go.
The amount that a sailor must learn quite appals,
    No wonder promotion is slow.

Such patience and fortitude, wisdom and tact,
    Such cool-headed judgement required,
The art to know just where and when how to act,
    You sailors may well be admired.

I've learned many things since I first went aboard
    Which I hope I shall never forget,
With nautical knowledge my mind has been stored,
    But there's heaps that I want to know yet.

Alas 'tis denied me, no longer around
    Thy galleys and decks may I roam,
Thy head lies to seaward, due south thou art bound,
    And in less than five weeks will be home.

Then farewell, *Iberia,* here though I stay,
  Still to thee my heart ever is true.
A new set of passengers thou must convey,
  But they will not love thee as I do.

When far o'er the pampas I scour the plain,
  My thoughts will turn often to thee;
Though on horseback, in fancy, I'll live o'er again
  Those five happy weeks on the sea.

Ah, there goes the signal, well "Goodbye, old friend,"
  They are heaving the port anchor fast.
"Haul down the Blue Peter," so this is the end,
  Don't forget me, I'll wave 'till the last.

Adios, dear ship, with a full heart and eye,
  Do I follow thy watery track;
Take my love to old England, and once more, "Goodbye,
  "God speed thee, and bring thee safe back."

During a voyage in the Orient liner "Orontes" Sir Alan Herbert is believed to have received a direct hit from a passing seagull. It is said, but it cannot be proved, that he immediately wrote the following lines which then found their way to Lieut-Commander K. C. A. MacKenzie who gave them to Capt R. G. C. Riley who gave them to "Sea Breezes". Apart from their intrinsic merit they show that the rivalry between the Orient Line and P&O also extended to passengers.

  O seagull I'm grieving to find you relieving
    Yourself on the Merchant Marine.
  I presume you've good sight and can see by this light
    That *Orontes* is not a latrine.

  God gave you the oceans for your little motions,
    And Italy offers a Po,
  But if it is finer to aim at a liner,
    Then why not a nice P&O?

"Sea Breezes", August, 1946.

The Little Ships
by J. S. Beattie

Gallant British coasters,
   Dunkirk to Normandy,
Fighting off the bombers
   To keep the channels free.
Blowing from the west'ard,
   Bombs from the enemy,
Mines in the Channel,
   And E-boats from the sea.

Guernsey Queen, London Queen,
Nivernais, Teeswood,
Glengarriff, Gwenthills,
Ortolan and *Jim,*
Carnalea, Aseity,
Skelwith Force, Monkwood,
Seaville, St Angus,
Channel Queen and *Grim.*

Gallant British coasters
   Backing up the landing,
Pouring out of London
   With Plimsol-covered freights,
Loaded with munitions
   And bombs for the handling,
Boring down to Dover
   Then facing through the Straits.

Asteria, Gladonia,
Durwood, Kaida,
Beachfield, Brackenfield,
Galacum and *Queen,*
Antiquity, Aridity,
Southport, Plasma,
Cordale, Aviedale,
Romeo and *Sphene.*

Gallant British coasters,
   Bringing up the bacon,
In at every landing,
   With fighting men and guns,
Feeding Allied nations
   Everything is taken
In little British coasters
   By gallant British sons.

Waldo Hill, Eilean Hill,
Sollund, Ebrix,
Rockville, Avanville,
Kylegorm and *Spes,*
Runnelstone, Monkstone,
Tudor Queen, Robrix,
Foreland, Zealand,
Clara Monks and *Tres.*

"Sea Breezes", April, 1948.

British Coasters
by Eric Minett

Though only small ships — not given to boast,
Few parts are strange around this old coast;
Shetland to Skerries, Solway to Start,
Every creek, every cove from the Dee to the Dart
   Is known to the brave British coaster.

Of their comings and goings little is known,
The Channel's their workshop, this coast is their own;
Labouring along they may roll round the Lizard,
Find the Foreland in fog or Cape Wrath in a blizzard.
   'Tis the way of the brave British coaster.

From Cardiff with coal for Bantry Bay,
To Preston from Par with white china clay.
Every headland they know, each set of the tide
Swirling swift thro' the Pentland, playing tricks on the Clyde.
   All the same to the brave British coasters.

Unlike their big sisters that sail the deep seas,
Built for big cargoes or the passenger's ease;
"The liner's a lady" — someone has said,
The coaster's no breeding, but courage instead.
   They need it, these brave British coasters.

What will we find in the little ship's hold?
Not bars of bright silver nor ingots of gold,
But tons of "black diamonds" and good golden grain;
That's the little ship's cargo, again and again.
   The lifeblood of brave British coasters.

In summer and winter, in sunshine or snow,
Whatever the weather, the little ships go
Chugging down-Channel in fog or a gale;
'Tis seldom they falter, rarely they fail.
   They've got guts, these brave British coasters.

And what are the names of these brave little ships?
How homely they sound and soft on the lips;
There's *Coral* and *Cushag*, *Ben Veen* and *Ben Ain*,
Broomfield and *Briar*, *Gem*, *Jesmond* and *Jane*.
   Soft sounding for hard British coasters.

What of the men who man these small ships?
Few sea lawyers' yarns escape their salt lips,
But they'll tell you the course from the Shipwash to Spurn,
Of the soundings off Sligo they've little to learn.
    The schooling of brave British coasters.

Maybe you'll forgive the coaster to boast
Of the part that they played off the Normandy coast,
But there's nothing too much — nothing they'd shirk
Which they proved beyond doubt in that "epic" Dunkirk.
    Salute then, the brave British coaster.

God speed you on, all you brave little ships,
A prayer from the heart through a landlubber's lips;
May the billows be bright and soft breezes blow
To help and not hinder as you pass to and fro.
    All honour to all British coasters.

"Sea Breezes", January, 1924, attributed to "G.V."

The Steamer

With rigid lines and box-like form
    The steamer onward presses,
Shows neither fear for raging storm
    Nor wish for winds' caresses.

The force that drives her o'er the main
    Within her hull is working,
Each crank and piston bears its strain
    Of forward, backward jerking.

No sails are spread to catch the breeze,
    But with its ceaseless turning,
The driving screw churns up the seas,
    Their mighty forces spurning.

When tempests howl and waters crash,
    Now lifting, now depressing,
Her way she keeps with dip and splash,
    With measured speed progressing.

No beauty does she claim, or grace
    In movement, shape, or bearing,
But storm or calm she keeps her pace
    With man her duties sharing.

"Sea Breezes", January, 1949.

At Gravesend

by W. J. King

Down they come in smart succession,
Saturday afternoon's procession,
Outward bound to oceans wide,
Making the most of every tide.

Stately liners, Orient bound,
Coasters small, for Plymouth Sound,
Ballast collier going to Tyne,
To fill with product of the mine.

Short-sea traders for the north,
Scottish coasters for the Forth,
Black-funnelled Continental trader,
Staunch, as Tyneside shipwright made her.

Lines and rigs of varied modes,
Big Plate tramp for Barry Roads,
Round to Mersey, round to Clyde,
Baltic, Humber, and Tees-side.

We may be thankful we have these,
Carrying our trade across the seas,
Pray Heaven watch them as they go,
And we remember what we owe.

The "Clan Shaw" was built by the Greenock Dockyard Co and started her maiden voyage on January 25, 1950. Capt B. M. Leek discovered these anonymous verses in a copy of "Shipping World" and incorporated them in his description of the ship in "Sea Breezes" in March, 1988.

The *Clan Shaw* is a wonderful ship
   Which is sailing early this year
From Greenock, the town where she was built,
   To ports both far and near.

She has a great array of derricks on her masts
    And a radar also fitted on a tower;
We hope that as long as foreign trade lasts
    She will sail the seas with power.

Her Parsons reaction turbine is well made,
    She has a funnel with a helmet at the top;
All this has been fitted by Messrs John J. Kincaid
    From their well-known engineering shop.

She has 16½ knots when she is at sea
    Which is exactly 19 miles per hour;
A great propeller this is bound to be
    To provide 10,340 shaft horsepower.

She carries 12 passengers on each run
    And both builders and owners should be complimented
For all the difficult work which they have done
    And experimented.

There are other ships to follow her for Clan Line
    And I will finish now their names to state:
The *Clan Sinclair*, and another just as fine,
    The *Clan Sutherland* at a later date.

"Sea Breezes", October, 1921. In sailing ship days it was the practice to screw in as many bales of wool or cotton as possible, sometimes almost to the detriment of the safety of the ship which might literally burst at the seams. It was said of Capt Richard Woodget that he could get into the "Cutty Sark" a thousand more bales than any other master. This poem was attributed to "Brady".

You can dunnage casks of tallow, you can handle hides an' horn,
You can carry frozen mutton, you can lumber sacks o' corn;
But the queerest kind o' cargo that you've got to haul and pull
Is Australia's staple product — is her God-abandoned wool.
For it's greasy an' it's stinkin', an' them awkward, ugly bales
Must be jammed as close as herrings in a ship afore she sales.
    For it's twist the screw and turn it,
    And the bit you get you earn it,
You can take the tip from me, Sir, that it's anything but play
    When you're layin' on the screw,
    When you're draggin' on the screw,
In the summer, under hatches, in the middle of the day.

"Sea Breezes", November, 1949.

The Channel for Orders

by Wilfred H. Scott-Shawe

Our barque, the *Falls of Garry*,
Was built of iron and steel,
Her four masts were two hundred feet
From painted trucks to keel.
Her homeward run from 'Frisco
Was the fastest made by sail.
From the island of Mauritius
She had carried the ocean mail.

They loaded her with golden wheat
At Port Augusta's quay;
We beat her down the Spencer Gulf
'Till we reached the open sea,
We ran the roaring easting down,
In five and thirty days,
To that grim outpost of the Horn,
Diego Ramirez.

The green seas swept her both fore and aft,
On the tail of the Burdwood Bank;
The weed grew thick as a mermaid's hair
On teakwood and pitchpine plank.
Higher the Great Bear swung in the sky
And low sank the Southern Cross
As we left behind us the storm-tossed seas
And the haunt of the albatross.

Out from our beam came the South-East Trades,
And we merrily bowled along,
As we trimmed our yards to the welcome breeze
Each lifted his voice in song;
Then we warmed our limbs in the sun's hot rays
As we dried out our sodden gear;
Our bags and sea-chests we daubed with paint,
For the end of the voyage seemed near.

But the wind dropped light in the Doldrum belt,
And we drifted across the Line
In longitude thirty and seven west,
When our days out were fifty-nine.
We swung the yards to each breath of air
'Mid the heat and the tropical rain;
Then the wind would fly to the other beam,
And we'd swing them around again.

The booby sits in the futtock shrouds,
The grampus blows on our lee,
The gulf weed lifts to the gentle swell
As far as the eye can see,
The bosun-bird circles overhead,
With his marlinespike of a tail.
Then the longed-for breeze fills the weather leach
And we heel to the pull of the sail.

When abreast of the Western Islands
The Trade winds all died away;
We dipped our rails in the ocean swell,
Becalmed for a night and a day.

But when the westering sun sank down
In a darkening bank of clouds,
A stiffening breeze from the west-sou'-west
Came whistling through the shrouds.

The port watch squares the crossjack yard,
The starboard squares the main,
We loose all three topgallantsails;
The wind is fair again!
The helmsman keeps away a point,
That every sail may draw.
The Lizard now lies right ahead,
A thousand miles or more.

When running for the Channel, after sailing round the world,
With deep-sea lead kept handy, the royals neatly furled,
When from the spinning log-reel there flies the thirteenth knot
To drop into the foaming wake, how happy is our lot.

Forgotten are the hours of toil, the hardships we have borne
In the fierce heat of tropics or in winter off the Horn;
For there ahead lies England, beloved of all lands,
With leafy lanes and rolling downs, cool mists and golden sands.

He who has never strayed away far from his own homeland
Cannot know the joy seamen feel, he would not understand
The thrill that moves the hardiest one when, like some star, the light
Gleaming upon that outpost rock, the Bishop, heaves in sight.

Beyond the lights of Scilly the Wolf Rock stands forlorn.
The Lizard is the next we sight, and, with the rosy dawn,
Against the skyline there appears, white in the light of day,
Those pyramids of gleaming sand from Austell's china clay.

We heave-to when abreast the Rame, with mainyard all aback;
To call the cutter on our lee, we hoist the pilot jack.
They lower a boat, there comes on board the man with local skill,
Who, having rapped his orders out, away again we fill.

We haul her close off Penlee Point, then reach towards the fort;
All hands stand by to go about; we leave the Knap to port.
Then "Hard-a-lee, let fly head-sheets!" and as they come aback,
The after yards are swung and we fill on the starboard tack.

And standing into Cawsand Bay, all hands then shorten sail,
Each mans a topsail downhaul, a leachline or a brail.
When Eddystone is shut away by Penlee's wooded steep
The anchor's let go with a splash in seven fathoms deep.

The sails are stowed, the ropes coiled down, the watch has gone below.
Then one by one the lights shine out ashore on Plymouth Hoe,
From off the land the evening breeze steals gently o'er the bay,
Laden with the scent of gorse, wild thyme and new-mown hay.

The moon beyond the Mewstone
   Rock displays her beauty calm,
And country sounds are faintly heard
   from Maker's woodside farm,
The plaintive cry of straying lamb,
   the barking of a dog.
"Arrived, all well, in ninety days"
   is entered in the log.

The *Falls of Garry* will race no more,

Home bringing the golden wheat.
Her passage from 'Frisco of days
   four score
There's never a ship will beat.

The conger lurks in her lazarette,
Her shrouds in the kelp weed trail,
In the rock-strewn bay where her
   fate she met,
By the steep Old Head of Kinsale.

The "Falls of Garry" was built at Greenock in 1886. She was sold in 1911 while homeward bound from Australia to Ireland, her purchase price of £3,450 being subject to safe arrival, but the vendors never collected. In thick fog on April 26 she ran aground on Quay Rock, off Ballymacus Point, Ireland. All her crew were taken off safely but the ship was too badly damaged to make salvage possible and she was left to go to pieces where she lay.

"Sea Breezes", August, 1924, attributed to "G.V.".

The Crewless Wireless Craft

In days long past the paddle played its part in forward motion,
Soon challenged by the spreading sail unfurled on every ocean.
Large fleets propelled by coal-made steam for distant ports were loaded;
While others gained their impetus from mineral oil exploded.

Electric power invisible, compact, its force expended;
A few short years its generous help to floating homes extended,
But now (we speak in time not yet, prophetic is our vision)
The crewless, wireless ship we view (waste not your swift derision).

Today with myriad cathode rays, atomic forces splitting
Electron speed to unseen craft are from the land transmitting,
A tube in shape, no deck, no keel, no funnel, ventilator,
No rudder, engine, mast or screw, nor even navigator.

Controlled by gyroscope its course, through aerial wave connected,
From port to port across the seas unshackled yet directed.
If solid matter in its path should threaten to destroy it
Its telepathic sentient powers on courses new deploy it.

Till, as the distant port is neared, the waiting tuned receiver
In action fixes guiding "wave" by tapping key and lever.
If weakly bolt or rivet false should cause the tube to founder,
The magnet will attract and with galvanic powers surround her.

So here we have the future ship, unloseable we deem her,
No longer need we navigate with paddle, sail or steamer.

"Sea Breezes", July, 1922, attributed to "G.V."

Homeward Freights

Tell me, Master, of your cargo,
   What it is, and whence;
Whether near of if you far go,
   Earning pounds and pence!

Tell me of your steaming, sailing,
   Of the storms you meet,
Of the seas behind you trailing
   On your lengthy beat.

Over seas, serene, terrific,
   West and south and north,
Channel, Strait, the great Pacific,
   Have we ventured forth.

Dashing on thro' seas gigantic,
   Decks agleam with brine,
Thro' the stormy, cold Atlantic,
   O'er the sun-scorched Line.

Under deck, in bag and packet,
   Varied goods are stowed;
While the engines, with their racket,
   Haste us on our road.

Nitrate, grain, from temperate Chile,
   Many curious seeds,
Are from plain and regions hilly
   Brought to fill your needs.

Oil and cotton, sugar grainy,
   Gold and copper, too,
Gather we from valleys rainy,
   Tropical Peru.

Cocoa, coffee — Ecuadorean,
   Fibres, tagua, bark,
Dyes and drugs and fruit arborean,
   Lie within our ark.

Silver, tin, and metals varied,
   Dug from mines Bolivian,
In the depths since ages buried,
   Wrested from oblivion.

Boundless fields of Argentina
   Fill our holds with maize;
Southern straits and Isles Malvina,
   Wool and tallow raise.

   So we drive across the ocean,
     Sail or steam or oil
   Moves us on in constant motion,
     For your food we toil.

Reprinted from a photocopy of a page from an unidentified magazine. From some of the phrases used it would appear to be American in origin.

The Other Man's Loss is My Gain

I'm a cargo surveyor, a checker and weigher
I separate, sort and compare
The stained and the sound, with my ear to the ground
For misrepresentations, take care!
I boss the longshoremen, a dozen or more men
Drop hooks when they see me pass by,
For "Handling in Transit" how anything stands it
Is surely a wonder, say I!

There's rumour of shipwrecks, there's oil in the 'tweendecks,
There's salt water, fresh water, brine,
There's contamination, too much fermentation,
And leakage in ten casks of wine,
There's copra that's rotten, six bales of wet cotton,
Crude rubber, raw sugar and grain,
A ship is on fire — just what I require,
The other man's loss is my gain.

An overturned truck is a great piece of luck,
A worm-eaten barge is my meat!
A smothering-line with a leak is divine,
As are ship-sweat, and dampness and heat,
Spontaneous ignitions — all damage conditions,
Some matting infected with lice,
And flour with weevils and all sorts of evils,
And coffee with inherent vice.

Some fruit overripe, and some old rusted pipe,
Men's shirts, chocolate, candy and soap,
Some toys in transhipment, electric equipment,
And coils of the finest hemp rope,
Some pilferage in cases of Chantilly laces,
A carton of damaged canned milk,
A statue for church, and a long futile search,
For the cause of some damage to silk.

Some lumber that's green, the worst that I've seen,
Split peas, and some long Chinese hair,
A shipper pernickety, antiques very rickety,
Shoes that I just cannot pair!
Irate consignees, and some maggots in cheese,
Some shrimp for Japan, packed in ice,
Some damage by hurricane, sisal that's wet by rain,
Pockets of damp, swollen rice.

There's beetseed that's mildewed, some olives quite ill-hued,
A harp, and some moth-eaten books,
A rug from Damascus, a fake if you ask us,
That's damaged by stevedores' hooks,
A cargo-surveyor! A life that is gayer,
You really must search far to find,
With trips out of town that I never turn down,
Though a hundred odd jobs trail behind.

For the G.A. adjuster, my forces I muster,
To minimise loss I sweat blood,
I squeeze the last dollar, though retailers holler,
The markets with off-grade I flood,
I salvage wet carbon black, poke at a bag that is slack,
Climb over mountains of scrap,
I help stow some big sedans, look at some leaking cans,
Finding what caused the mishap.

There's heat that's intense, there is smoke that is dense,
And holds that are darksome and deep,
And jobs late at night when it's really a fight,
To ward of some much needed sleep,
Now I'm not complaining, I'm merely explaining,
The ins and the outs of my trade,
For take it or leave it, I like it, believe it,
It's one way of making the grade.

It says much for the perfection of this poem that although it has been published many times in a variety of newspapers and magazines, all versions are almost word-for-word the same. It appeared in "Sea Breezes" in June, 1946 (the only version for which a date can be given) but of all the copies available only one is attributed and it is therefore this version which is given here. The poem takes the form of a letter from a shipowner's cargo claims manager to a shipper who has claimed that his goods were damaged in transit.

Shipowner's Cargo Liabilities

by L. H. Rowley

It is much to be regretted
That your goods are slightly wetted,
But our lack of liability is plain.
For our latest Bill of Lading,
Which is proof against evading,
Bears exception for sea water, rust and rain.
Also sweat, contamination,
Fire and all depreciation,
That we've ever seen or heard of in a ship.
And our due examination,
Which we made at destination,
Shows your cargo much improved by the trip.
Furthermore, the Protest shows,
That the Master blew his nose,
But the hatches were demolished by the gale.
Oh, we'll ever stick together,
To prove it's heavy weather,
For we cannot have the dog wagged by its tail.
'Tis a cause of grief sincere,
And we almost weep to hear,
You are claiming for your cargo wet by rain.
It really is a crime,
That you're wasting all this time.
For our Bill of Lading clearly makes it plain,
That from ullage, rust or seepage,
Water, sweat or just plain leakage,
Act of God, restraint of Princes, theft or war,
Loss, damage or detention,

Lock-out, strike or circumvention,
Blockade, interdict or loss twixt ship and shore,
Quarantine, or heavy weather,
Fog and rain, or both together,
We're protected from all these and many more,
And it's very plain to see,
That our liability,
As regards your claim is absolutely nil.
So try your underwriter,
He's a friendly sort of blighter,
And is pretty sure to grin and foot the bill!

This letter is said to have provoked the cargo shipper into replying:

Our reaction to your letter
Would have been a good deal better
Had you offered to accept our modest claim,
And regardless of excuses
(Which seem open to abuses)
We must still hold you exclusively to blame.
You talk glibly of the clauses
Which can cover all the causes
Of the damage suffered in the present case,
But if given careful study
You will find that all the ruddy
Things are only put in there to fill up space.
'Tis a very well known fact
That the clauses that are packed
In a Bill of Lading are not all quite binding.
Exemptions now can be no more
Than in the Act of '24
And of this you should have needed no reminding.
But to leave the legal side,
Where the case is open wide,
We've had plenty of cargo coming by your ships.
You know we're the biggest shippers
Of our brand of carpet slippers
And presently you'll find you've had your chips.
Either meet our claim in full
Or we'll ship our stuff by Hull
And ask our friends to try and do the same.
And if we should succeed,
For a fleet you'll have no need,
And you'll know you've only got yourself to blame.

At least one insurance company official took the injunction "So try your underwriter" to heart and attempted a settlement by arranging a meeting between the parties and then writing to each in turn. These verses are said to have been in circulation in the 1950s and are attributed to Mr R. G. Wareing of the Liverpool office of the Maritime Insurance Co Ltd.

To The Shipowner

It's our pleasure to advise you,
Though this hardly will surprise you
That the cargo owner's claim we've promptly paid
And with this liquidation
We have taken subrogation
And a study of your verses we have made.
The defence which you've expounded
Has apparently been founded
On a basis unacceptable in law.
For the true cause is not stated,
You have merely tabulated
A schedule of exceptions by the score.
In the contract of affreightment
There's an undisputed statement
That the Hague Rules override the printed text
And the loss was estimated
On the quay, then truly stated
On the very day of landing, or the next.
Now it seems to us mysterious
That an effect so deleterious
Could arise without your negligence or blame,
For you very well must know that
Prima facie proof's established of the same.
The lower you try to put it
You have no facts to rebut it
So you now must reconsider your defence.
There's no ground for litigation
Nor yet hope of mitigation
So you must us reimburse for our expense.
As there can be no objection,
And you've no valid protection
From the weather unexpected in its force,
Our debit note's appended
So the matter can be ended.
Your remittance we await in early course.

To The Shipper

We are only underwriters
And your claim does not affright us,
As our single aim and object is to pay.
That is what we're here for
And our rates you'll not think dear for
Our eagerness to make the hay.

When the sun and moon together,
Not to mention stormy weather
And a leaky, squeaky vessel badly stowed,
Cause your merchandise to suffer
With dirty water from the scupper
And seepage from a smelly keg of wood.
Then we gladly take the onus
And present you with a bonus
For the steamer is immune by Act of God;
While the friendly underwriter
Turns both cheeks to the smiter,
Who works on him that other act (of cod).

If the stuff when shipped was awful
It's inherent vice of jawful
We may think the pigeon isn't ours.
Still we like to please our friends
And we haste to make amends,
We pay our claims with money and with flowers.
When the goods vamoose through pilfer
And the shipper sends a bill for
A risk that none but fools would scorn in Asia,
Though the policy declares,
It's the shipper's risk not their's,
The underwriters smile and pay *ex gratia*.

Oh it's a lovely kind of life
For a writer and his wife
When he takes to underwriting for a living,
But as his shares decline from par
He has got to go and live with Ma
Whilst the merchant and the shipper go on thriving,
So this, the only, information
He sends abroad to clients in every clime,
The rates must be withdrawn,
(For his pants are now in pawn),
The premium shall be made to fit the crime.

"Sea Breezes", November, 1920, attributed to "G.V."

Nautical Nausea

The man who sails to foreign lands
    Forgets his Mother tongue,
So in his jargon now I sing
    What ne'er before was sung.

The good ship locks out from the quay
    To pitch upon the seas;
Her forefoot cleaves the foaming waves,
    Her hands the ratlines seize.

Sometimes, while riding in the roads,
    She's driven on the shore;
But what she sheers off from the land
    Makes neither less nor more.

Her anchor from the stream is fished,
    A bight on either fluke;
But as the stock is lashed to bits
    It isn't fit to cook.

At each boom end doth swiftly run
    The strong upholding gin,
But tho' a sailor's fond of pegs,
    With this he wants a pin.

The crow's nest up the mast is perched,
    And nowhere near the hatch;
The painter often may be foul,
    The sea-cocks never scratch.

A package does not fly thro' air
    When sent ashore in slings;
Nor is the cargo lighter when
    They take it from the wings.

Don't try to puzzle what this means,
    Its sense you'll never track;
But let the shellbacks cruise and feed
    Upon the same old tack.

All Aboard

As I stood on the bridge at midnight,
A thought came into my head:
Why the Hell am I standing here,
When I could be at home in bed?

By an unknown Second Mate.

The late Fred G. Shaw believed that this parody of Rudyard Kipling "If—" first appeared in the magazine "Wireless World" about 1913 and included it, from memory, in an article about his life at sea in "Sea Breezes" in November, 1970.

The Wireless Operator

If you can keep your nerve when all about you
    Are stations jamming hard and blaming you;
If you can "hold the air" though others flout you,
    Until you get your longest message through;
If you can send and not grow weary sending,
    Nor overtire the man who has to read;
If your mistakes are rare but prompt their mending,
    If you believe that haste is never speed.

If you can contemplate the chatter,
    Of greenhorn operators fresh from school;
If you can sit with messages that matter
    And wait until they've finished, and keep cool;
If you can read through half a dozen stations
    The weaker signals that are meant for you
And pick them out with few interrogations,
    Yet never feel ashamed to ask those few.

If you're a Jack of all Trades, tinker, tailor,
    If there is scarce a thing you cannot do;
If you're an electrician and a sailor,
    Telegrapher, accountant, lawyer, too;
If you're propelled by energy that's tireless,
    If you don't fear a job that's never done,
Then take my word, you're fit to work at wireless,
    And anything you get, you'll earn, my son.

Origin unknown, submitted by Capt R. G. C. Riley.

When first I was Apprentice I often did pretend
That when I got promoted I would be a seaman's friend,
But in a little longer I got to be a Mate
And soon like many others quite forgot my former state.
When I became a Captain I thought myself a King
And never did remember the Apprentice I had been.

"Sea Breezes", April, 1924.

The Purser

by Greville E. Matheson

Imposing in his uniform,
   With gold on sleeves and cap,
His tact is inexhaustible,
   And constantly on tap;
A very courteous gentleman,
   "A jolly decent chap!"

You would not tell *him* that
   he's fat —
Unless you'd give offence —
But it is clear that he is fed
   Regardless of expense,
And by his Line he's classed
   among
   Their best advertisements.

His cabin is a pleasant place,
   With portraits everywhere,
It's evident he's many friends,
   And mostly young and fair;
If not a wife in every port —
   Well, sweethearts here and there.

He's fond of asking friends to tea
   Inside his cosy den,
At times he's talked with princes
   there,
And chummed with famous men;
And as you pass his door you hear
   His cheery voice, "Say when".

He does some work, but marking
   time
Appears to suit him best;
He has a thin mysterious book
   He calls a manifest,
It's useful when he's tired of play
   And feels he wants a rest.

For then he'll slowly bring it forth,
   And with a shrug of woe,
He'll murmur, "Beastly shame,
   you men,
"So sorry, don't you know,
"Important work, er, must
   be done,
"Afraid you'll have to go."

His popularity on board
   Is, like himself, immense;
He never gives himself away,
   He never gives offence;
He's Mrs Winslow's Syrup mixed
   With heaps of common sense.

These lines, attributed to the late Sir Alan Herbert, were submitted by Mr Nelson French, formerly chief purser of the Orient liner "Orontes" and appeared in "Sea Breezes" in October, 1987.

   Yes, that is the purser with lots of gold lace,
     And nothing whatever to do;
   Not an officer really, but quite a nice face,
     And matters immensely to you!

"Sea Breezes", July, 1923.

The Chief Steward

by Greville E. Matheson

The Captain of a liner is
   A most important man,
He's been a haughty autocrat
   Since liners first began;
But tho' he rules upon the bridge,
   He's but an empty show —
The C.S. is the actual man
   That makes the ship to go!

The officers are splendid chaps
   To work the ship and crew,
As keen as mustard to excel
   In all they have to do,
But are they indispensable
   On board a steamer? No! —
The C.S. is the actual man
   That makes the ship to go!

The engineers are clever folk,
   And experts in their way,
Their life is one of constant toil,
   With very little play,
But tho' they work by day and night,
   And risk their lives below —
The C.S. is the actual man
   That makes the ship to go!

He's pushful, but he's tactful, too,
   He calmly goes ahead,
The kind of man who sidles in
   Where angels fear to tread.
And I maintain, without a doubt,
   Without irreverence,
The C.S. is the actual man
   That bosses Providence!

A statement from the Board of Trade that there was nothing to prevent a woman from "following the sea" prompted an unknown poet to submit the following contribution to the "Daily Courier", from which it was picked up by "Sea Breezes", March, 1923. The verse owes much to the lyric written by Sir W. S. Gilbert for the opera "HMS Pinafore".

   I'm the Captain of the *Pinafore*,
      And a right good Captain, too.
   I'm very, very good, and be it understood
      I command a right good crew.

   Yes, my pinafore's been scrapped since I earned the title "Capt"
      And I've done with hats and frocks.
   Can you see me? Well, you may, if you'll toddle down to-day
      To the landing-stage or docks.

   Let me add that to a man, all my crew are spick and span
      In their reefer-coats (and pants).
   This most wonderful of crews I must really introduce —
      As my sisters and my cousins and my aunts!

According to Denis Griffiths, who included it in his book "Power of the Great Liners" (Patrick Stephens Ltd, 1991), this poem graces the control-room bulkhead of the "Queen Elizabeth 2" and can also be found in the engine-rooms of many other ships.

Tribute to the Forgotten Man

The siren shrieks its farewell note, and proudly on her way
The brand-new giant liner moves in grandeur down the Bay.
A marvellous creation, her builders' joy and pride,
The great hope of her owners as she floats upon the tide.
The passengers in festive mood, 'mid laughter, jest and quip,
With keen delight enjoy the great ship's maiden trip.
She's sure to break the record, she'll do thirty knots or more,
Is the hope of all on board as she leaves her native shore.

Upon the bridge the Captain, a skipper proud and bold,
Bedecked in glorious raiments, navy blue and gold.
All eyes are fixed upon him, and it's going to his head,
He stops to drop the pilot, then rings "Full speed ahead!".
And "down below" the battle starts for the trophy of the seas,
By engineers, not clad in gold, but greasy dungarees.

On deck the scene is bly and gay, fair ladies, song and wine,
But hell is popping down below, beneath the Plimsoll Line.
The Chief raps out his orders to the men on watch below.
His men obey his mandates, about their tasks they go.
Steam pressure must not fluctuate, the bearings not run hot,
Revs must not be allowed to drop to make the thirty knots.
At dinner on the first night out the Captain proudly boasts:
"We'll surely break the record," as the gallant ship he toasts.
But breaking records puts no grey hair upon his head,
His contribution ended when he ordered "Full ahead".

Through weary days and sleepless nights to consummate his dream
The engineers slave ceaselessly till Ambrose Light's abeam.
The record has been broken with thirty-one point four,
The Captain wears another stripe, he's now a Commodore.
And thus he gets the credit for what other men have done
He boasts to press and radio the victory he has won.
Neglecting e'en to mention as he swings his ballyhoo
The men of brain and brawn and guts, who shoved the great ship through.

The moral of this poem then is quite conclusively,
The glory seldom goes to those who win the victory.
So keep this simple thought in mind about a record trip,
The man behind the throttle is the man who drives the ship.

"Sea Breezes", May, 1946, unattributed.

The Skipper and the Engineer

The Skipper and the Engineer
  Had fussed throughout the trip,
Their arguments were loud and clear:
  "Who runs this blooming ship?"

"It takes good brains to navigate,"
  The Skipper roughly said,
"Or engineers would be fish bait
  "Down on the ocean bed."

The Engineer with eyes agleam
  Replied without a flinch:
"Whenever I turn off my steam,
  "You cannot steer an inch."

The Skipper roared: "Look here, you snob,
  "A dollar to a dime,
"That I can run your blinking job
  "But you can't tackle mine."

The Engineer said: "That's a go,
  "Give me your cap and coat,
"And you take mine and go below,
  "And I will steer the boat."

They switched their jobs and each one swore
  While cigarettes they lit,
In just about an hour or more,
  He'd make the other quit.

While on the bridge the Engineer,
  Enjoyed the cool sea breeze,
The Skipper breathed an atmosphere
  Bedewed with oil and grease.

The day's routine seemed just the same,
  For all was going well,
When up on deck the Skipper came,
  And started raising hell.

"Damn you!" he yelled, "I had to quit,"
   As on the bridge he darted.
"Your engine's stopped and I'll admit,
   "I cannot get it started."

The Engineer just turned around
   And gave a hearty laugh.
Said he, "Old top, we've been aground
   "For three hours and a half."

Writing in "Sea Breezes" in December, 1946, Mr Bernard Berenson, of Washington, USA, asked for a copy of this poem which, he said, he first saw tacked to a bulkhead in the steamer "Laurel" in June, 1929. This version was given in the magazine in February, 1947. A variation said to have been seen aboard an American ship has the title "Mr Fall Guy", the verses in a different order and some words altered.

Call the Mate

If the running lights go out, call the Mate,
If your latitude's in doubt, call the Mate,
If the wind begins to howl, if the sailors start to growl,
If the whistle lanyards foul, call the Mate.

If you're coming into port, call the Mate,
If the midnight lunch runs short, call the Mate,
If the cargo starts to shift, if the workboat goes adrift,
If the fog begins to lift, call the Mate.

If you want to drop the hook, call the Mate,
If you're looking for the cook, call the Mate,
If you run a light abeam, if the Chief can't give you steam,
If the mess-boy has no cream, call the Mate.

If you need the crew on deck, call the Mate,
If the gangway is a wreck, call the Mate,
If the capstan's on the blink, if a load falls in the drink,
If you don't have time to think, call the Mate.

If the ship begins to roll, call the Mate,
If the cook runs out of coal, call the Mate,
If the Old Man goes to bed, if you see a squall ahead,
If you need a sounding lead, call the Mate.

Yes, that's who the fool guy is, it's the Mate,
All the pretty girls are his — ask the Mate.
And sh! that poor old bird never gets a pleasant word,
Thank God I'm just the Third, not the Mate.

*The American version has another verse, updated to take account
of refrigerated containers, and completely upsets the last verse:*

If the boxes won't defrost, call the Mate,
If the chartroom key is lost, call the Mate,
If the windlass doesn't work, if the reefers go berserk,
If the night mate is a jerk, call the Mate.

Yes, that's who the fall guy is,
All the pretty girls are his,
That poor old bird never gets a pleasant word,
Thank the Lord I'm only Third, not the Mate.

"Sea Breezes", July, 1924.

A Ship's Doctor
by Greville E. Matheson

A mail boat "Doc", tradition says,
   Is a tremendous swell,
He does but little all his days,
   But does that little well.

For doctors in due course to slay
   Their scores is not a crime;
He has no chance, his *metier*
   Is simply killing time.

His bunkside manner's most urbane,
   He beams with sympathy
The while he orders dry champagne,
   Or sal-volatile.

His social gifts are quite unique,
   His dancing is divine,
At auction, when his hand is weak,
   His play is super-fine.

At entertainments he is great,
   At concerts he's the star,
And you should hear him imitate
   A cat or motorcar!

He strolls about engagingly,
   "And *how* are *you* to-day?"
For while the sun is shining, he
   Believes in making hay.

So tho' he flirts with much resource,
   He flirts with tact and care,
Resolved to marry in due course
   Some widow rich and fair.

"Sea Breezes", September, 1923.

The Modern Skipper

by Greville E. Matheson

Altho' he's now *non est,* the ancient kind —
   The "old sea-dog" I'm told the proper term is —
Yet scratch the modern skipper, and you'll find
   That he is, underneath his epidermis,
About the same in nearly every way
   As was the skipper of a bygone day.

He's still a roving eye, when on the quay
   Or in the street he spies a pretty maiden,
No matter where, at Plymouth or Portree,
   At Porto Rico, Mossel Bay or Aden,
He's still — in his platonic way — as fond
   Of any pretty girl, brunette or blonde.

Altho' he is, perhaps, more dandified,
   More prone to patronise a West End tailor,
He's still as genial and as free from side,
   He's every whit as keen and good a sailor,
As cool and bold, when stormy winds do blow,
   As was his predecessor years ago.

Altho' he is more polished than of old,
   Renowned, it may be said, for his urbanity,
Whereas the old-time skipper, so I'm told,
   Was better known for his profanity,
Altho' the modern skipper does not swear —
   Except at times — the discipline's still there!

And on the whole, altho' the ancient skipper
   Has "gone aloft" — I'm told the proper term is —
Yet scratch the modern skipper, and you'll find
   That he is, underneath his epidermis,
As good a sailorman as any man
   Since first the Mercantile Marine began.

"Sea Breezes", April, 1923.

Instructions to Captains

by Greville E. Matheson

The members of a steamer's crew
   Are most important folk,
When tired of work they should not be
   Obliged to do a stroke;
Convey to them in kindly tones
   It's well that they should rest,
Provide deck-chairs and cigarettes
   Or *Murias* of the best.

If any of them feel unwell,
   Just treat each case with care,
X-rays and other things should be
   Forthcoming then and there.
And if a fireman has catarrh,
   Or pain inside his stom____
(Beg pardon!) give him arrowroot
   And port *ad libitum*.

Provide light reading for their use,
   Bentham, or Donne, or Mill,
Chemin de fer, and Put and Take
   Or other games of skill.
If any of them yearn for quoits,
   For cricket or hopscotch,
You should arrange accordingly,
   And let them off their watch.

If deck-hands choose to take French leave,
   And slip on shore at night,
You must not chide them, but explain
   Such conduct is not right.
Arrange a lecture, if you can,
   With lantern slides to show
That beer has not the qualities
   Possessed by H_2O!

If trimmers should refuse to trim
   Or greasers fail to grease,
You should not drive them or adopt
   The methods of police.
Just take them gently, one by one,
   And say a text or two,
Or start a hymn — and the effect
   Is sure to startle you!

Submitted to "Sea Breezes" by Mr J. H. MacLean, of Oban, who found the lines in an autograph book signed by Ewan McGwerion, December 2, 1919. It is not known whether Mr McGwerion composed the lines or simply quoted them from another source. They almost certainly refer to the "Titanic" disaster of 1912 in which the owner, Bruce Ismay, was saved while the master, Capt E. J. Smith, went down with his ship.

The Captain stood where a Captain should,
   For the law of the sea is grim;
The owner romped as his boat was swamped
   And no law bothered him.

The Captain stood where a Captain should,
   When a Captain's boat goes down,
But the owner led when the women fled
   For an owner must not drown.

The Captain sank as a man of rank,
   While his owner turned away,
The Captain's grave was his bridge, and brave
   He earned his seaman's pay.

Aids to Navigation

When in danger, never fear,
You can always blame the engineer.
                    By another unknown Second Mate.

The present International Regulations for the Prevention of Collision at Sea had their genesis in Part V of the Merchant Shipping Act, 1894. Known informally as "The Rules of the Road", they were devised under the leadership of Thomas Gray, head of the Marine Department of the Board of Trade, but it was Gray himself who composed the following rhymes for the benefit of candidates for certificates of competency as navigating officers. Some of the verses have since been rendered obsolete by a change in the method of issuing helm orders.

The Rules of the Road
by Thomas Gray

When both side lights you see ahead,
Port your helm and show your red.

Green to green or red to red,
Perfect safety, go ahead.

If to your starboard red appear
It is your duty to keep clear;
To act as judgement says is proper,
To port or starboard, back or stop her.

But when upon your port is seen
A steamer's starboard light of green,
There is not so much for you to do
For green to port keeps clear of you.

"Sea Breezes", February, 1946, reprinted from an issue of the General Steam Navigation Co's "News Letter". The company's ship "Gannet" was in collision with the "Wendy" in 1924, the subsequent court case being heard by Mr Justice Langton. The "News Letter" recorded that the judge wrote the following summary of the case and gave it to GSN chairman Mr W. J. McAlister.

The *Wendy* and the *Gannet*
  Were in the cold North Sea,
The *Gannet* struck the *Wendy*
  And they brought the case to me.

The *Wendy* showed her green light
  And the *Gannet* showed her red,
And the Master of the *Wendy*
  Gave the order: "Full ahead!"

The Master of the *Gannet*
  Was filled with deep disgust
And the wind within his bowels
  Was a swift and spiral gust.

He viewed the nearing *Wendy*
  With the gravest of concern,
And in an anxious moment
  Crammed his engines full astern.

    My sad but painful duty
      Is to put them both to shame,
    For neither kept the crossing rule,
      So both ships are to blame.

"Sea Breezes", July, 1949.

Navigation
by H. M. Atkinson

The modern navigator who squares the root of "A",
   Is doubtless very clever in his ultra-modern way,
He knows the sines and tangents, that "A" squared equals "B",
   And "XYZ" is nothing until multiplied by "C".

He can prove by twisted angles that a circle is a square,
   A line is really nothing, never reaches anywhere,
And believes he's born expressly to tell old sailors why
   God put the stars and planets in their places in the sky.

By "triggy" rules he demonstrates the Skipper's just a fool,
   And over his deficiencies he'll pass the sliding rule.
The Old Man doesn't worry, goes smiling on his way,
   Deriving consolation from the thoughts of yesterday.

For the modern seamen's fathers sailed the oceans far and near
   When they hadn't Sperry gyros or patent steering gear;
And the log, the lead and lookout played an all-important part
   When they did their navigation on a darned old Blueback chart.

But the old men seemed to get there just as safely as today,
   With their prehistoric methods, in their prehistoric way,
And the records left behind them most indubitably tell
   That the modern navigator may be proud to do as well!

Capt S. T. S. Lecky was the author of a book which became a standard text for deck officers, "Wrinkles on Navigation". As he was also a master with the Pacific Steam Navigation Company the editor saw no harm in reprinting his wrinkle on weather forecasting in the June, 1921, edition of "Sea Breezes".

January to March:
   Snowy
   Flowy
   Blowy

July to September:
   Moppy
   Croppy
   Poppy

April to June:
   Showery
   Flowery
   Bowery

October to December:
   Breezy
   Wheezy
   Freezy

These verses were found in "Sea Breezes" archives marked "East Coast rhymes. File under 'Miscellaneous'". They are given here in the same form as the original typescripts but some also appeared, slightly different again, in a series of readers' letters in "Sea Breezes" in 1962 and were said then to date from the turn of the century.

East Coast Rhymes

From Blackwall Reach we make our way,
   Down London River to the sea so grey.
At Gravesend Pier the pilot goes ashore,
   So "Full speed ahead" down to the Nore.
We take a last long look
   At the dear old Kentish shore.

The old North Sea has a heavy swell,
   And our engines race merrily as well,
Our firemen are busy down below,
   As the thick black smoke from our funnels flow.

There's an old collier on our lee,
   Looks like the old *Wynyard Park* to me;
We will beat her, don't you see,
   She is the slowest collier on the old North Sea.

Our bosun cheerily reads the log,
   A steady ten knots, he tells the Mate,
As at the Tyne Dock piers
   We should not be late.

Eight bells is struck, the watch is o'er,
   Our sailors rush to the fo'c'sle door,
The wind is whistling, the tide is strong,
   But our gallant old collier goes pelting along.

We pass the Shipwash on our way,
   West-nor'west is Hollesley Bay,
Our Skipper says: "We are quite all right,
   "We soon will see the Orford light."

The night is clear, the moon is bright,
   Off Southwold Pier, the coast we sight.
Two long low colliers are heading south,
   One wonders who they will be,
Two of Cory's ships, no doubt,
   The old *Nellie Wise* and the *James Joicey*.

Off Lowestoft Ness some drifters pass,
    Homeward bound from sea;
What homely names they seem to have,
    Two Sisters, Friendly Girls, Welcome Home,
Willing Boys and *Honey Bee.*

A rusty tramp comes steering south,
    Down to the Plimsoll loaded,
She proves to be the old *John Ray,*
    Bound out of Barcelona.

Another collier is heading south,
    Bound for the London River
I know she is the *Stewarts Court*
    Owned by Lord Londonderry.

Our lookout sights the Cortin light,
    Gorleston cliffs are on our lee,
Through Hewett's Channel we steam along,
    And pass the famous Scoby.

Through Yarmouth Roads, at break of day,
    We pass the Cockle on our way,
Then the Dudgeon, then the Spurn,
    Flamboro' Head comes next in turn.

Flamboro' Head as you pass by,
    Filey Brigg is drawing nigh,
Scarboro' Castle stands out to sea,
    Whitby high light bears northerly.

Huntly Point, that very high land,
    It's five and twenty miles from Sunderland;
And our Old Man says: "If things go right,
    "We will be in Tyne Dock by midnight tonight."

✳ ✳ ✳

Northbound

When it's high water at London Bridge,
    It's half ebb at Swin;
When it's low water at Yarmouth Roads,
    It's half flood at Lynn.
First the Dudgeon, then the Spurn,
    Flamborough come next in turn;
Filey Brigg is drawing nigh,
    Scarborough Castle stands on high;

Whitby Rock stands out to sea,
　So steer two points more northerly.
Huntcliffe Foot is very high land,
　Twenty-five miles to Sunderland.
Hartlepool lies in the bight,
　Seaham harbour is now in sight.
Skipper says: "If the weather's bright,
　"We'll be in Shields this very night."

Southbound

Roker, Whitby, Flamborough, Spurn,
　Outer Dowsing next in turn,
East Dudgeon and Cromer bold,
　Look out for Haisborough and the Wold;
Then Kentish Knock, the Goodwins three,
　North, East and South in turn you'll see.
Then Dover with its cliffs so white,
　Dungeness is now in sight.
Beachy and Owers, stream the log,
　Down the Channel, clear of fog.
Point to point and light to light,
　We'll sail along both day and night.

*　*　*

Start Point to Beachy Head
　Tell their tale of quick and dead;
Forelands both to Dungeness
　See many ships in dire distress.

The Lizard and the Longships know
　Of the end of friend and foe,
And many and many a seaman's knell
　Has been rung by the Manacles' bell.

Gull and Dodman ask aright,
　A wide berth on a dirty night;
Bolt Head and Bolt Tail
　Are ill spots in a Channel gale.

Overnight to Portland Bill,
　In Channel fog it's just as ill;
And Wolf Rock and Seven Stones
　Rest their feet on sailors' bones.

But from Nore light to Cape Cornwall,
　Goodwin Sands are worst of all.

Space permits only three variations of this well-known aide-mémoire for North East Coast navigators.

> First the Dudgeon, then the Spurn,
>   Flamborough Head stands next in turn,
> Scarborough Castle standing high,
>   Whitby Rocks are drawing nigh,
> Hartlepools lie in the bight,
>   We'll have a pint in Shields tomorrow night.

※ ※ ※

> First the Dudgeon and the Spurn,
>   Flamborough Head comes next in turn,
> Whitby light stands on a height,
>   Forty-two miles from Tynemough light.

※ ※ ※

> First the Dudgeon, then the Spurn,
>   Flamboro' Head comes next in turn,
> Whitby Castle stands out to sea,
>   Twenty-seven miles right northerly.
> Sunderland town lies in a bight,
>   Thirty-six miles from Whitby high light.
> The Old Man says: "If all goes right
>   "We'll all get drunk in Shields tonight."

A seaman's version of the 23rd Psalm was submitted by Mr Julian Holt, of the Blue Funnel Line family, and was published in "Sea Breezes" in December, 1990. The lines were recognised by Capt Idwal Pritchard, of Holyhead, as those written by John H. Roberts in 1874 and it is this version which is given here.

The Pilot Psalm

The Lord is my Pilot, I shall not drift; He lighteth me across the dark waters; He steereth me in deep channels; He keepeth my log; He guideth me by the Star of Holiness, for His Name's sake.

Yea, though I sail 'mid the thunders and tempests of life, I will dread no danger, for Thou art near me; Thy love and Thy care they shelter me.

Thou preparest a harbour for me in the Homeland of Eternity; Thou anointest the waves with oil, my ship rideth calmly. Surely sunlight and starlight shall favour me on the voyage I take, and I will rest in the Port of God for ever.

Envoi

No man will be a sailor who has contrivance enough to get himself into a jail, for being in a ship is being in a jail with the chance of being drowned . . . A man in a jail has more room, better food and commonly better company.

Boswell's *Life of Johnson*

Culled from the newsletter of the North Russian Convoy Club, Auckland, New Zealand, who lifted it from a publication called "Up Spirits" who seem to have got it from someone in the Royal Navy who was familiar with the works of John Masefield.

    I must go down to the seas again,
        it's not that I want to go,
    But I found a chit on the table
        which told me it must be so.
    And all I ask is a billet snug
        and a nice little day-work job,
    Many decks from the boiler plates
        and the mighty turbine's throb.

    I must go down to the seas again,
        to a gay little foreign port,
    Where women and gin and original sin
        are the favourite local sport;
    And all I ask is a cabaret girl
        and a quart of synthetic Scotch,
    A friendly patrol to bring me off
        and a chum to stand my watch.

    I must go down to the seas again
        (though I'd rather stop on the beach),
    So steer a course for southern climes,
        far from Stuka's reach;
    And all I ask is a fortnight's pay,
        a song, a girl and some wine,
    And a refit in Durban that lasts
        until the lights of London shine.

    Then I will go back to the beach again
        and never a wistful sigh
    Shall cross my lips as I think of ships
        or the wind and the seagull's cry;
    And all I ask is a cosy fire
        and a wife and a pub next door,
    Where I'll sit and drink and make them think
        that through me we won the war.

Titles (in italic) and First Lines

A Ballad of the "Ortega"	34
A "Larri" boat from Barry Dock	20
A mail boat "Doc", tradition says	63
A Sailor's Bill of Fare	14
A Ship's Doctor	63
A Song of the Sea	17
A Stentorian "If-"	32
Altho' he's now *non est*, the ancient kind	64
All up and down the oceans and by the cottage fires	21
An Old Shellback on His Life at Sea	26
As I stood on the bridge at midnight.	55
At Gravesend	42
British Coasters	40
Call the Mate	62
Down they come in smart succession.	42
East Coast Rhymes.	71
Esso our help in cargoes past	33
Farewell to the "Iberia"	36
First the Dudgeon, then the Spurn	74
From Blackwall Reach we make our way	71
Gallant British Coasters	39
Have you ever been aboard a tramp.	19
Have you stood on a bridge at midnight	24
Homeward Freights.	47
I must go down to the seas again, it's not that I want to go.	77
If the running lights go out, call the Mate	62
If you can earn your leave and start to take it.	32
If you can keep your nerve when all about you.	57
If you can keep your wines within the limit	15
If you'll listen for a while I will tell you a tale.	22
I'm a cargo surveyor, a checker and weigher	48
I'm on one of Hungry Houston's ships.	12
I'm the Captain of the *Pinafore*	59
Imposing in his uniform	58
In days long past the paddle played its part in forward motion	46
In eighteen hundred and thirty-one, I first set out to sea.	26
Instructions to Captains	65
It is much to be regretted.	50
It's our pleasure to advise you	52

January to March	79
	70
Laden deep from lands afar	30
Landing Craft, Infantry	31
"Liberty" Ship	30
Maggie May	22
Monday comes and while upon the seas	14
Nautical Nausea	54
Navigation	70
O seagull I'm grieving to find you relieving	38
O what's the use of grumbelling, you know you get your whack	11
Ode to Tramp Steamers	29
"Old Hardy" of the Seamen's Mission	21
Our barque, the *Falls of Garry*	44
Our reaction to your letter	51
Passengers and mail can go by Wells Fargo	27
Roker, Whitby, Flamborough, Spurn.	73
Shanghaied in San Francisco	16
She's a wonderful ship, through the sea she will flip	31
Shipowner's Cargo Liabilities.	50
Start Point to Beachy Head	73
Tell me, Master, of your cargo	47
The Captain of a liner is.	59
The Captain stood where a Captain should	66
The Channel for Orders	44
The Chief Steward.	59
The *Clan Shaw* is a wonderful ship	42
The Company's "If-"	15
The Crewless Wireless Craft.	46
The Laws of the Merchant Navy	9
The Laws of the Merchant Navy are intrinsic, pithy and plain	9
The Lay of the Merchant Navy	23
The Life of an AB.	16
The Little Ships	39
The Lord is my Pilot, I shall not drift.	74
The man who sails to foreign lands.	54
The members of a steamer's crew	65
The modern navigator who squares the root of "A"	70
The Modern Skipper	64
The Old Whalerman's Song.	18
The Other Man's Loss is My Gain	48
The Pilot Psalm.	74
The Purser	58
The Rules of the Road	69

The ship she was a British ship, the Union Jack she flew. . . 34
The siren shrieks its farewell note, and proudly on her way. . . 60
The Skipper and the Engineer. 61
The Skipper and the Engineer 61
The Steamer 41
The *Wendy* and the *Gannet*. 69
The Wireless Operator 57
Though only small ships — not given to boast. . . . 40
'Tis well nigh sixty years ago 18
Tramps, tramps, tramps — aye, by the thousand. . . . 29
Tribute to the Forgotten Man 60

Voyage of the "Honorius", 1919-21. 12

We are only underwriters 53
We live on scupper nails and bread 25
When both side lights you see ahead. 69
When first I was Apprentice I often did pretend. . . . 57
When in danger, never fear 67
When it's high water at London Bridge. 72
Whether wine is in or wit be out 17
Wistfully silent I stand on the quay 36
With rigid lines and box-like form 41

Yes, that is the Purser with lots of gold lace 58
You can dunnage casks of tallow, you can handle hides an' corn . . 43
You'll do no good by grumbling, you know how well you're whacked. . 11
You've seen him in the street, rolling round on groggy feet. . . 23